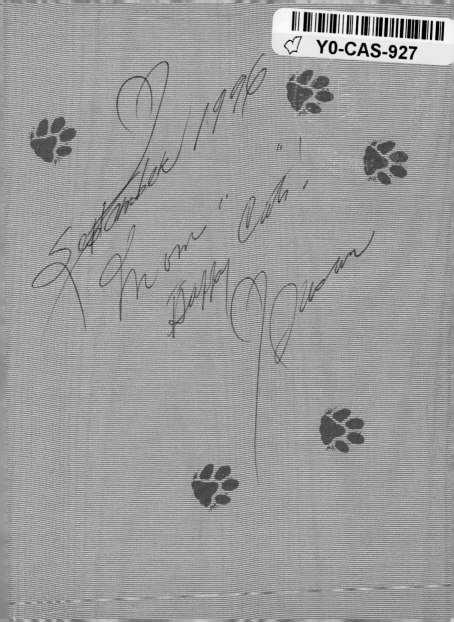

September 1996

From "Cats"

Betty Buckley

THE
CAT'S
MEOW

THE
CAT'S
MEOW

Edited by Kevin Osborn

Ariel Books

Andrews and McMeel

Kansas City

ISBN: 0-8362-4722-1

Library of Congress Catalog Card Number: 94-71131

The text of this book was set in Joanna.

Design by Chris Welch.

10 9 8 7 6 5 4 3 2

CONTENTS

INTRODUCTION 7

THE HISTORY OF THE CAT 11

CAT CULTURE 15

CAT FANCY AND
  CATS NOT-SO-FANCY 21

TO A CAT 27

CAT TALK 29

CAT TALES 39

Introduction

What is it about cats? No other animal arouses such passionate responses: People either love them or hate them—not that it matters in the least to the Cat. Yet the supremely indifferent Cat permits no indifference among the humans who share its world. Where cats are concerned, there is no middle ground. And cats probably prefer it this way. Though they don't really care how anyone feels about them, they like to know where they stand.

Cats are the least domesticated of house pets. Yet despite (or because of) their inherent wildness, cats are the most beloved of pets. Those who love them, love them passionately. Americans own nearly sixty million cats. All right, perhaps no one owns a cat—but sixty million have deigned to share our homes.

Why do more Americans embrace cats than any other pet? The answers are here. Kittens—playful, energetic, mischievous, comical, curious creatures—awaken the child in us, bringing out our own senses of wonder and adventure. Grown cats—mysterious, graceful, independent, alert, contemplative, and wild—touch our souls, reaching into the depths of our spirit to restore our appreciation for beauty and silent wisdom.

Moody, indifferent, superior, disdainful, and affectionate (or not), the Cat does not make friendship an easy affair. Oh, kittens make friends with humans easily enough. But as they grow older, they disdain the easy familiarity with which they once related to creatures as inferior as humans. (Could it be that cats are ashamed to associate with us? Possibly—except of course that cats feel no shame.) To relate to a cat, you first have to win its respect, not to mention its affection. Developing a relationship with a cat, a beast that refuses to be tamed, is like working at a marriage. Yet like a marriage, the loving interplay between people and cats offers more rewards, more intimacy, than relationships with other

THE HISTORY OF THE CAT

The Evolution of the Cat

Befitting their reputation for survival against all odds, cats have a long and storied history. The cat family apparently evolved from the same ancestors as contemporary mongooses and civets. Fossils of the cat family date back about forty million years. However, the oldest known fossil similar to today's cats is around twelve million years old. One of the earliest of the modern mammals to evolve, the crafty Cat has survived virtually unchanged for the last ten million years. So in evolutionary terms, cats are older than we are. Perhaps this is one source of their feelings of superiority.

Domestic cats comprise just one of almost forty different species of cat. To zoologists, cats fall into one of three genera:

• *Felis*, the smaller, purring cats, ranging from the mountain lion to the domestic cat;

• *Panthera*, the larger, roaring cats, including the lion, tiger, leopard, and jaguar; and

• *Acinonyx*, the speedy cheetah, the only cat whose claws do not retract.

Of these, only the felidaes (*felis catus*—or "felix the cat") have been domesticated—or rather, have consented to domestication.

Most of today's domestic cats probably descended from the Caffre cat, a breed still found today in Syria, Egypt, and throughout Africa. This wild cat of Africa was the first that chose to live near people. Not that they had any particular desire to consort with people. No, what drew cats to join human communities was not people themselves, but rather the hordes of rats and mice attracted by their stores of food. Opportunistic cats saw human communities as offering the promise of an easy life: an abundant and accessible source of fresh meat. In turn, people welcomed these rat killers, the ancestors of all domestic cats, for protecting their grain.

The word quickly spread. From Egypt and Africa, domestic cats were introduced to control rodent populations in Europe and Asia. Within the last few centuries, settlers introduced domestic cats to North America, South America, and Australia. Among the seven continents, only icy Antarctica remains catless today. And small wonder: What self-respecting cat would put up with that kind of cold coupled with the absence of the creature comforts it has come to expect as its birthright?

CAT CULTURE

Despite their economic value as ratcatchers and their emotional worth as companions, cats have not always had an easy time in human company.

The relationship started out regally. The ancient Egyptians, who first domesticated cats at least four thousand years ago, not only welcomed cats for protecting their grain, but actually revered the Cat. Venerating the Cat as a sacred being, the Egyptians developed cat cults and temple worship of cats. They believed that gods took the shape of cats in order to convey omens and commandments to the people. (The cats naturally took this to heart, endorsing and adopting as their own the belief that they were indeed gods.) Ra, the sun-god, changed himself into a cat in order to battle evil. Bast, the goddess of fertility and love, always took the form of a cat—or at least the head of a cat attached to the body of a woman. The ancient city of Bubastis was her chief seat of worship.

The Egyptians prized the Cat so much that they imposed the death penalty for any killing of a cat, even accidentally. By law, families who mourned the loss of their cat had to shave their eyebrows as a sign of their grief. Dead cats were often embalmed and mummified—and even furnished with embalmed mice for their dining pleasure in the after-life. These mummified remains, tomb paintings, and statues, some dating back forty-five hundred years, provide the earliest evidence of domesticated cats. In the ruins of one ancient city, more than three hundred thousand mummified cats were discovered!

The Egyptians who first recognized the pleasures of the domestic cat were not eager to share their discovery. Yet despite a ban on the export of cats, Phoenician traders eventually smuggled tame cats to Europe and the Orient. About 500 B.C., the Greeks, too, finding themselves unable to obtain cats from the Egyptians through trade, stole some to control the mouse population. The descendants of these illicit felines, sold to Romans, Gauls, and Celts, soon spread throughout Europe.

Also around the fifth century B.C., cats began appearing in China. Sanskrit writings provide evidence that domestic cats guarded grain in India no later than 100 B.C. The Japanese, however, did not begin to appreciate the wonders of the Cat until another seven centuries had passed.

The Roman Empire helped the Cat conquer Europe. As the influence of Rome spread throughout Europe, so did the influence of the domestic cat. Many Roman conqueror carried cats with them as a symbol of liberty. Although most Europeans introduced to the Cat recognized their value in reducing the population of rats, mice, and other rodents, few appreciated the godlike qualities that the Egyptians had revered. Only in Scandinavia, where two cats pulled the chariot that carried Freya, the Norse goddess of love and beauty, were cats recognized as divine creatures. This lack of human recognition did not, of course, cause cats to renounce their god-hood. They continued to regard themselves as deities—and to disdain those humans who blindly ignored their divinity.

Though few in Europe accepted the Cat as a god, many began to regard it as a demon. The

Middle Ages were truly the Dark Ages for cats. Condemned as symbols of paganism, witches' familiars, and agents of Satan, cats were persecuted and nearly wiped out by the fifteenth century. The extermination of cats undoubtedly helped rats to spread the murderous Black Death: the plague that between 1347 and 1351 killed twenty-five million Europeans, one-fourth of the population. Although a handful of visionaries continued, as the Egyptians had before them, to revere the cat for its supernatural qualities, the scattered practice of cat worshiping ended in Europe at the end of the fifteenth century. Under orders from Pope Innocent VIII, the Spanish Inquisition burned thousands of these "pagans" at the stake.

Fortunately for cat lovers, the Cat apparently does have nine lives, for it not only survived this systematic persecution, but won new respect and admiration. In the wake of yet another plague, the Great Plague of London, seventeenth-century Europeans gained a renewed appreciation for the Cat's skill at destroying disease-infested rats. Around 1750, cats were introduced to control the rodent population in the American colonies. By the end of the century, cats had once again established their place (on the hearth, with their backs to the fire) in homes throughout Europe and America. And the rest, as they say, is history.

CAT FANCY AND CATS NOT-SO-FANCY

The vast majority of cats are mongrels—not the product of selective breeding, but of midnight caterwauling. Though mongrel cats are both more popular and more populous than show cats, however, the United States alone stages more than four hundred cat shows, featuring only the finest breeds of cat, every year.

Cat exhibitions began in Europe over four centuries ago. Although cats were at that time still valued primarily for their rat-catching abilities, people began taking great pride in the unique characteristics of their cats (alas, the reverse was seldom true). By the mid-nineteenth century, the breeding of cats, the progressive refinement of desirable qualities, had begun. Although the cats would probably have been content to keep their virtues to themselves, cat owners understandably wanted to show them off. As a

result, the first modern cat show, featuring two dozen show classes, was held in London in 1871. Four years later, Edinburgh, Scotland, saw its first cat show. And by 1895, the U.S. had imported cat fancy, holding the first American cat show at New York's Madison Square Garden.

Why breed cats? Certainly not, as dogs are bred, to improve their hunting or other skills. Generations of domestication have actually diminished the cat's hunting skills, which are passed on primarily through observation of the mother's hunting. No, cat fanciers breed cats for only one reason: To enhance and purify their already considerable beauty. To attain the ideal of feline beauty, cat fanciers have bred more pleasing head and body shapes; softer, glossier, longer coats; and, above all, purer and more eye-catching colors in both coats and eyes.

Cat fanciers have developed so many new colors and types of cats that contemporary cat shows judge nearly one hundred different classes, with new ones introduced almost every year. The two major divisions of cats are the long-hairs and the shorthairs. Longhairs, by far the most popular breed among cat fanciers, are all Persians. (The amount of care and grooming longhairs demand, however, makes them less popular than shorthairs among cat owners who do not enter cat shows.) Classed according to color, Persians span the rainbow and beyond. Show classes of longhairs include: white, cream, black, blue, red, chinchilla (silver), shaded silver, smoke (black, white undercoat), brown tabby, silver tabby, blue tabby, red tabby, tortoiseshell (black, orange and cream), calico (black, red-orange, and

cream), blue-cream, shell cameo, shaded cameo, smoke cameo, tabby cameo, and Himalayan.

Shorthairs come in six main breeds: Siamese, Abyssinian, Burmese, Russian Blue, Manx, and domestic. The Siamese are judged in four breeds: seal point (seal-brown points—i.e., face, ears, legs, and tail), chocolate-point (chocolate-brown points), lilac-point (grayish-pink points), and blue-point. Abyssinians come in ruddy, red, and blue varieties. The varieties of Burmese include brown, milk-chocolate brown, champagne, platinum, blue, sable, and lilac. Manx varieties include black, tortoiseshell, bicolor blue, blue-cream, and white with blue eyes.

To the cat fancier, every physical characteristic of a cat brings a special delight: the cat's unique body shape, the pointed or rounded shape of the head, the quality of its fur, the vivid color of its eyes, the dramatic shift in color that defines a Siamese's points, and the silky softness, vibrant color, and glossiness of its coat. All these features are taken into account by cat show judges as well. (Of course, a cat's disposition, as all cat lovers know, is not subject to human judgment.)

The term *cat fancy* perfectly captures the spirit of breeding and showing cats. A powerful fancy for cats motivates those who breed and show cats. And the cats, too, are fancy indeed: They exhibit a beauty and purity seldom found in more ordinary domestic cats. Nonetheless, whether fancy or plain, pedigreed or not, all cats have their own particular beauty, fascination, and charm—especially to their owners. Fancy that.

To a Cat

Stately, kindly, lordly friend,
  Condescend
Here to sit by me, and turn
Glorious eyes that smile and burn,
Golden eyes, love's lustrous meed,
On the golden page I read.

All your wondrous wealth of hair,
  Dark and fair,
Silken-shaggy, soft and bright
As the clouds and beams of night,
Pays my reverent hand's caress
Back with friendlier gentleness.

Dogs may fawn on all and some
  As they come;
You, a friend of loftier mind,
Answer friends alone in kind.
Just your foot upon my hand
Softly bids it understand.

—*Algernon Swinburne*

CAT TALK

No matter how much cats fight, there always seem to be plenty of kittens.

—Abraham Lincoln

A kitten is chiefly remarkable for rushing about like mad at nothing whatever, and generally stopping before it gets there.

—Agnes Repplier

There is no more intrepid explorer than a kitten. He makes perilous voyages into cellar and attic, he scales the roofs of neighboring houses, he thrusts his little inquiring nose into half-shut doors . . ., he gets himself into every kind of trouble, and his always sorry when it is too late.

—Jules Husson Champfleury

But buds will be roses, and kittens, cats,—more's the pity!

—Louisa May Alcott

Time, that spoils all things, will, I suppose, make her also a cat. . . . For no wisdom that she may gain by experience and reflection hereafter will compensate for the loss of her present hilarity.

—William Cowper

Everything that moves, serves to interest and amuse a cat. He is convinced that nature is busying herself with his diversion; he can conceive of no other purpose in the universe. . . .

—F. A. Paradis de Moncrif

The real objection to the great majority of cats is their insufferable air of superiority.

—P. G. Wodehouse

If you are worthy of his affection, a cat will be your friend but never your slave. He keeps his free will though he loves, and will not do for you what he thinks unreasonable; but if he once gives himself to you, it is with absolute confidence and fidelity of affection.

—*Théophile Gautier*

A cat is there when you call her—if she doesn't have something better to do.

—*Bill Adler*

If I called her she would pretend not to hear, but would come a few moments later when it could appear that she had thought of doing so first.

—*Arthur Weigall*

When we caress her, she stretches herself and arches her back responsively; but this is because she feels an agreeable sensation, not because she takes a silly satisfaction, like the dog, in faithfully loving a thankless master.

—*François René de Chateaubriand*

Cats always know whether people like or dislike them. They do not always care enough to do anything about it.

—*Winifred Carriere*

My cat does not talk as respectfully to me as I do to her.

—*Colette*

As every cat owner knows, nobody owns a cat.

—*Ellen Perry Berkeley*

A cat cares for you only as a source of food, security, and a place in the sun. Her high self-sufficiency is her charm.

—*Charles Horton Cooley*

Most cats, when they are Out want to be In, and vice versa, and often simultaneously.

—*Louis J. Camuti*

Did St. Francis really preach to the birds? Whatever for? If he really liked birds he would have done better to preach to the cats.

—*Rebecca West*

Cats find malicious amusement in doing what they know they are not wanted to do, and that with an affectation of innocence that materially aggravates their deliberate offense.

—*Helen Winslow*

The Cheshire Cat only grinned when it saw Alice. It looked good-natured, she thought: still it had *very* long claws and a great many teeth, so she felt it ought to be treated with respect.

—*Lewis Carroll*

Most of us rather like our cats to have a streak of wickedness. I should not feel quite easy in the company of any cat that walked about the house with a saintly expression. . . .

—*Beverly Nichols*

When my cats aren't happy, I'm not happy. Not because I care about their mood but because I know they're just sitting there thinking up ways to get even.

—*Penny Ward Moser*

We should be careful to get out of an experience only the wisdom that is in it—and stop there: lest we be like the cat that sits on a hot stove-lid. She will never sit down on a hot stove-lid again—and that is well; but also she will never sit down on a cold one any more.

—*Mark Twain*

By associating with the cat one only risks becoming richer.

—*Colette*

. . . Purring beside our fireplaces and pattering along our back fences, we have got a wild beast as uncowed and uncorrupted as any under heaven.

—*Alan Devoe*

The phrase "domestic cat" is an oxymoron.

—*George Will*

... The Woman laughed and said, "You are the Cat who walks by himself, and all places are alike to you. You are neither a friend nor a servant. You have said it yourself. Go away and walk by yourself in all places alike."
Then Cat pretended to be sorry and said, "Must I never come into the Cave? Must I never sit by the warm fire? Must I never drink the warm white milk? You are very wise and beautiful. You should not be cruel even to a Cat."

—*Rudyard Kipling*

Oh, cat; I'd say, or pray: be-ooootiful cat! Delicious cat! Exquisite cat! Satiny cat! Cat like a soft owl, cat with paws like moths, jeweled cat, miraculous cat! Cat, cat, cat, cat.

—*Doris Lessing*

Calvin's life seems to me a fortunate one, for it was natural and unforced. He ate when he was hungry, slept when he was sleepy, and enjoyed existence to the very tips of his toes and the end of his expressive and slow-moving tail.

—*Charles Dudley Warner*

Cats are intended to teach us that not everything in nature has a function.

—*Garrison Keillor*

Her function is to sit and be admired.

—*Georgina Strickland Gates*

Cat Tales

Novelist Charles Dickens sat in his home reading one night by candlelight. When the candle went out, he set down his book, lit the candle once more, and briefly caressed his cat, whom he noticed looking up at him forlornly. He then returned to his book. Minutes later, Dickens's attention was drawn away from his book a second time. This time, he turned in time to catch the cat carefully snuffing the candle's flame with his paw. Once again, the cat plaintively looked up at Dickens through the dim light. The writer smiled gently, invited the cat into his lap, and with many warm strokes, rewarded the cat for his persistence and ingenuity.

A first-time guest at the White House in the 1920s viewed it as a great honor to share breakfast with President Calvin Coolidge. The guest so desperately wanted to make a good impression that he feared even the slightest violation of etiquette. The guest therefore followed his host's lead when he observed the president take his glass of milk and pour some into a saucer. Coolidge smiled at his guest's mimicry before silently leaning down and offering the saucer to his cat.

I was once told a pleasant story of an English cat who . . ., dozing one day before the nursery fire, was disturbed and annoyed by the whining of a fretful child. She bore it as long as she could . . .; then, finding passive endurance had outstripped the limits of her patience, she arose, crossed the room, jumped on the sofa, and twice with her strong soft paw, which had chastised many an erring kitten, deliberately boxed the little girl's ears,—after which she returned to her slumbers.

—*Agnes Repplier*, The Fireside Sphinx

A friend complained to humorist Dorothy Parker that his cat had gotten so ill that he had no choice but to put his beloved pet to sleep. Yet still he was torn: How could he possibly kill his closest companion? "Try curiosity," quipped Parker.